I give thanks to God for graciously sending people in my life who have encouraged me to write. Some of those people aren't even related.

I'm grateful to God for his Word. It's been life giving.

I'm thankful for Christ Point Church. It's been my great joy to serve as your pastor.

I'm humbled that the elders at Christ Point would not only give me permission to write, but cheer for me along the way. Thank you Billy, Phil, and Chris.

I thank God for friends like Brandon, Brian, Billy, and John. Over the last decade, God has used you to breathe life into me.

Thanks, Kim, for making this project better. I'm sorry if I made your red pen run out of ink.

Melissa, You're my person. I love you.

Introduction

God changes people. He does it all the time. He turns persecutors into preachers, scared fishermen into bold disciples, and crooks into Christ-followers. Even now he is changing you and me. One of the primary means that God uses to change us is his Word. With that in mind, I invite you to journey with me for 31 days through the book of 1 John. Read, reflect, and respond to the vastness of God's inexhaustible love. "See what great love the Father has lavished on us, that we should be called children of God!"

Day 1

"It Will Change your Life"

That which was from the beginning, which we have heard, which we have seen with our eyes, which we looked upon and have touched with our hands, concerning the word of life-the life was made manifest, and we have seen it, and testify to it and proclaim to you the eternal life, which was with the Father and was made manifest to us- that which we have seen and heard we proclaim also to you...(1 John 1:1-3)

My friend John often boldly declares, "*It* will change your life!" Through the years, "It" has been many things: a music subscription, a restaurant located in a pharmacy (I can't make this up), a stick-on wallet that attaches to your cell phone. I've tried each with various degrees of life-altering success. I will give him credit though; in each case, he speaks from firsthand experience.

If a friend told me, "Try this. It will change your life!" but he never tried it himself, I'd be skeptical. In 1 John 1, John makes it clear that he had experienced Jesus firsthand, and his life was now dedicated to sharing that with others. The disciples, who had firsthand knowledge of Jesus, thought him compelling enough to tell people, "Hey, you really should meet this guy! We've heard him teach. We've seen him with our own two eyes. We've greeted him—in flesh and blood. He changed our lives, and he will change your life." At the very least, it would make you consider a meeting.

The early followers of Jesus did not merely believe in the idea of Jesus or the hope of Jesus. They were believing, following, trusting, and telling other people about their firsthand experience with the reality of Jesus. They encountered him. They saw him. They walked with him. They listened to him. And then they, in turn, told other people about what they had experienced.

We don't experience Jesus the same way the disciples did. We don't shake hands, rub shoulders, high five, or dab with deity, but that doesn't mean we haven't met him. It certainly doesn't mean we don't know him or that we can't know him. In fact, by faith, we do know him. Jesus left behind a record of his life in the pages of Scripture, so we could know him. And because we know him, the life that was His is now ours.

If Jesus has changed your life because of your firsthand encounter with him, tell someone! Let him be the most important "It" experience you share with others.

The life was made manifest, and we have seen it, and testify to it and proclaim to you the eternal life

Reflect:

Have you met Jesus?
Who will you tell?

Day 2

A Place at the Table

That which we have seen and heard we proclaim also to you so that you too may have fellowship with us; and indeed our fellowship is with the Father and with his Son Jesus Christ. (1 John 1:2)

One day a friend called me and asked, "James, do you have a suit?" I was expecting a more traditional conversation starter. Something like, "Hey James, how are you?" But that's not what I got. "Yes, I have a suit." "Great!" my friend said, "Put it on and meet me downtown. Needing no further encouragement, I punched the address into my phone and found myself downtown at a rather large, unfamiliar building.

My phone buzzed. "Meet me at the top of the escalator," the text read. I found the escalator and stepped on. At the end of my ride, I looked up to see my friend standing there. "What in the world is happening?" I asked. "I have no idea why I'm here." My friend replied, "James, you're going to meet Joe Montana."

The Joe Montana? The Joe Montana of San Francisco 49er fame? Four-time Super Bowl-winning quarterback Joe Montana. NFL Hall of Famer Joe Montana! If you're not a football fan, you may not know Joe, but you should know I had lunch with him.

I stood in a room with a select group of very important people all waiting to meet the football legend. I still have the picture of him shaking hands with me. He signed a helmet for me. I had lunch with Joe that day. Well, me and a few hundred other people, but still, I was there. I was invited to sit at the table.

Do you know that you're invited to the table, too? Only the guest of honor is much more impressive, and the feast is much more satisfying.

Our fellowship is with the Father and with his Son Jesus Christ.

Fellowship is participation. We participate with the Triune God. Every day, no matter the time or place, you're invited to God's table. You may not know Joe, but you can know Jesus. The Trinity has put out a place setting for you, and your Redeemer, the guest of honor, is waiting. So come and feast.

Reflect:

What prevents you from meeting with God?
What would it look like for you to meet with him now?

Day 3

Joy Addict

And we are writing these things so that our joy may be complete. (1 John 1:4)

I'm addicted to joy, so it should come as no surprise that I pursue it at great cost. Just this last week, I can think of any number of decisions I made because I thought they would bring me joy. In no particular order:

> I ate an ice cream cone after lunch because I like the taste of ice cream even though ice cream doesn't always like me.
> I ate an ice cream cone after dinner for the same reason I ate one after lunch.
> I stayed up late to watch a game knowing I'd be exhausted the next day.
> I played a round of golf with a friend instead of getting ahead on some work.

I expected each decision to bring me a measure of joy. And they did! I loved the ice cream, I watched a great game, and I shot par on the 18th hole. I didn't walk away from those events disappointed with my joy, but I did find I wanted more of it.

God doesn't reject our pursuit of joy, but He does direct it. He shows us where joy is found. The Gospel of Luke records an event where an angel of the Lord says to the shepherds, "Fear not, for behold, I bring you good news of a great joy that will be for all the people. For unto you is born this day in the city of David a Savior, who is Christ the Lord." Joy has come and His name is Jesus.

When people think about Christianity, joy isn't always the first word that comes to mind. Rules, maybe. A lot of "Thou shalt not . . . ." But not joy. John, though, thought the idea was important enough to write to churches, so they would experience it. Can't you hear the joy in John's voice when he writes about his experiences with God in the flesh? Read 1 John 1:1-4 and see for yourself. As if in disbelief, he repeats over again that he is testifying to what the disciples had seen and heard, touched with their hands, and looked upon with their own eyes. It sounds like he's still pretty astounded that he had fellowship with Jesus. And his joy was made complete by sharing these experiences with the church, so that all believers could experience the same joy, not just in part, but more fully.

And we are writing these things so that our joy may be complete.

Today may you experience the fullness of God's joy for you in Christ.

Reflect:

Where have you looked for joy?
How successful were you in your pursuit?

Day 4

God is Light

This is the message we have heard from him and proclaim to you, that God is light, and in him is no darkness at all. (1 John 1:5)

I don't want to give you the impression I grew up in a cave, but the people who claimed me on their taxes weren't exactly guilty of driving up the electrical bill by leaving the lights on. The predominate chorus of my childhood, in no particular order, was:

1. Brush your teeth
2. To be early is to be on time; to be on time is to be late, and to be late is a sin
3. Turn off the lights!

I didn't like living with the lights off. I still don't. I've found when the lights are off, I can't see as well. Weird, I know. And when I can't see, I bump into things. And when I bump into things, I break things. Living in darkness is no fun. So, turn on the lights.

God is light. Light pierces the darkness. It illumines our path and exposes what is hidden. Light gives life.

God gives light to our path through his Word. He helps us see where we're going. Sometimes we'd like for Him to light our path for miles and miles. But often, he sheds light only on the next few feet—just enough to take the next step. That's usually all we need.

Light exposes what is hidden. Darkness in the Bible is often synonymous with sin, and sin is often practiced in secret. Jesus didn't mince words in John 3:20 when he said, "For everyone who does wicked things hates the light and does not come to the light, lest his works should be exposed." Light exposes this ugliness and helps us see truth. God brings light to dark places because God *is* light.

We're a mixed bag. We have some fine qualities, some admirable attributes, and some terrific character traits. But, we also have some embarrassing quirks, flaws, and foibles that we don't post on Facebook or Instagram. And underneath all those are the sins we try to keep hidden at the bottom of the bag We're a mixed bag, but God isn't. He is altogether beautiful.

God is light and in him there is no darkness.

What's amazing is that despite your quirks, flaws and sin, God's light is now shining through you. The light of God illuminates God's kids in such a way that other people take notice. God is light and in him, there is no darkness.

Reflect:
Has there been a time in your life when something that was in the dark was brought to light?
Is there anything in your heart or life that needs to be brought into the light?
What would it look like for you to expose what is hidden?

Day 5

Hand It Over

If we say we have no sin, we deceive ourselves, and the truth is not in us. If we confess our sins, he is faithful and just to forgive us our sins and to cleanse us from all unrighteousness. (1 John 1:8-9)

I'm not exactly sure when it happened, but some time after having children I became a professional caddy.

No, I don't hold their golf clubs. Instead, I find myself holding a whole lot of junk that doesn't belong to me: candy wrappers, empty cups, gently used pieces of gum, socks hot off sweaty feet.

I just stand there in disbelief thinking, "What do you want me to do with this stuff?"

We carry stuff around all the time that doesn't belong to us. Or, maybe it does belong to us, but it doesn't have to be carried by us.

Sin is baggage. It's a weight. It's like someone running with one of those weighted vests. Imagine doing that in Houston. . . in August. I've seen this crazy phenomenon, and usually I want to stop these people and gently remind them, "Sir, running is hard enough. There's really no need to carry that additional weight!"

If I didn't know better, maybe King David hung out in Houston? He writes about confession, "For when I kept silent…day and night your hand was heavy upon me; my strength was dried up as by the heat of summer" (Psalm 32:3).

David felt the heaviness of his unconfessed sin. It's out of touch with reality to deny we carry the heaviness of sin. It's like walking around with cookie on our face, but denying our hand was in the jar. John says we are only deceiving ourselves when we do this.

What do we do when we're carrying the weight of sin? Give it away.

If we confess our sins, he is faithful and just to forgive us our sins and to cleanse us from all unrighteousness.

Confession isn't a hocus-pocus magical spell that gets us out of trouble. Confession agrees with God that our thoughts, words, and deeds are contrary to his holy character. Confession joins with the tax collector who cries out to God, "Be merciful to me, a sinner."

The good news? When we confess, God removes the unnecessary weight. He is faithful and just to forgive us of our sins. It's in His character to do so. You can count on it. Are you carrying around unnecessary weight? Paul's words cheer us on: "Let us also lay aside every weight, and sin which clings so closely" (Hebrews 12:1).

Hand over all that extra weight to your Father.

Reflect:

Why is it difficult to actually admit our sin?

Is there sin in your life that God is calling you to give over to Him?
What's stopping you?

Day 6

Don't Do It

My little children, I am writing these things to you so that you may not sin. (1 John 2:1)

Many people believe the author of 1 John was an old man when he wrote this letter. He was likely your grandpa's age. I like grandpas. Grandpas have lived a little life. They've weathered the storms. They've seen fads come and go. Grandpas, at least godly grandpas, are full of wisdom. They offer advice that comes from personal experience. That is why when John writes, "I am writing these things to you so that you may not sin," I don't think he's doing it with a clenched jaw and a stern voice. I think he has experienced enough life to know that sin is never worth it.

Sometimes regrettable decisions in life are made in the heat of the moment. Your son or daughter drops your phone and the glass shatters. You're furious. Your blood boils. With voice raised, you say something you'd like to have back. Someone cuts you off on the way to work. They're texting and eating a breakfast sandwich, while simultaneously reaching in the back seat to grab their son's permission slip they forgot to sign. They drift into your lane. You immediately honk your horn, throw your hands to heaven, and spew out a few choice words. Those decisions happen in an instant.

Other regrettable decisions in life are well thought through. They're premeditated. Your spouse is working late. Your husband is out of town. Your parents put you in charge. Your boss is gone for a few days. You plot. You plan. You pretend. You prepare. You've determined to work your plan. No one will know. No one will notice. No one will find out. No one will get hurt. John, by now an old man, writes to remind us, "Don't do it. It's not worth it." It never is.

The purchase won't satisfy you.
The few clicks on the computer won't fulfill you.
The relationship won't complete you.

I am writing these things to you so that you may not sin.

John is testifying about Jesus knowing that the more a person understands the glory of the Son of God, the less attractive sin will appear. Sin will never be worth it.

Reflect:

Are you contemplating doing something that you'll regret?
What is it?
Tell someone. Remember, it's not worth it.

Day 7

Good News for When you Blow It

"But if anyone does sin, we have an advocate with the Father, Jesus Christ the righteous." (1 John 2:1)

I've blown it. I've lost my temper after committing to never again lose my temper. I've daydreamed of the good life after committing to a life of contentment free from the desire for more stuff. I've selfishly arranged my life to benefit me despite being inspired by verses about humility, selflessness, and service.

I'm going to go out on a limb and trust that I'm not the only one who has blown it. You have too. You've made choices in your life for which you wish you still had the receipt. You'd take it back in a New York minute. You'd do things differently. You'd choose wisely. But you can't. So, what do you do when you've blown it? Where do you turn? Go to God.

Remember John has just said he's writing to us so we may not sin, but knowing each of his readers will do that very thing, he provides the solution:

If anyone does sin, we have an advocate with the Father, Jesus Christ the righteous.

An advocate is someone who comes alongside you in times of need. Has there been a time when you've been in need? Of course! Significant challenges and difficulties in life confront us on a daily basis. Relationships. Parenting. Work. Health. Finances. The list goes on. All of these areas of need, while significant, pale in comparison to our spiritual need brought on by sin. Sin kills. The good news is we were never meant to face the fallout of our sin alone.

When we sin against the Father, we have an advocate with the Son, Jesus Christ.

In our guilt, we go to God.
In our shame, we reach out to our Savior.
In our regret, we cry out to the Righteous One.

Jesus is our advocate—a helper in our time of need.

Reflect:

In what ways do you need Jesus to be your advocate? Thank Jesus that he meets and helps in your time of need.

Day 8

Copy-Cat

By this we may be sure that we are in him: whoever says he abides in him ought to walk in the same way in which he walked. (1 John 2:5-6)

I have a few pet peeves. In no particular order:

1. I'm not a fan of people smacking their lips or making sounds while chewing gum. I think it's gross. When I see gum stuck to a table or a napkin, I throw up a little in my mouth.

2. It drives me absolutely batty when my kids look over my shoulder while I'm reading a text or an email. I want to remind my children that it's the parent's job to spy on their kids, not the other way around.

3. I just can't stand when my kids copy me. "Can you please pass the potatoes?" "Can you please pass the potatoes?" "How was your day?" "How was your day?" "Did you have a good day at school?" "Did you have a good day at school?" It's even annoying to write. Imagine how annoying it is to hear. Sometimes I'll get so frustrated that I yell, "Stop copying me!" Only to hear…wait for it…" Stop copying me!"

It may be annoying when my kids copy me, but we are called to copy Christ. In fact, one of the ways we demonstrate we know God is by copying His Son. We talk like he talked. We walk as he walked. We serve like he served. We love like he loved. We make it our aim to be a copycat. "For to this you have been called, because Christ also suffered for you, leaving you an example, so that you might follow in his steps (I Peter 2:21). So, go ahead, copy Him.

Reflect:

What marked the life of Christ?
In what ways does your way of life reflect his life?

Day 9

What's Love Got to Do with It?

Whoever says he is in the light and hates his brother is still in darkness. Whoever loves his brother abides in the light, and in him there is no cause for stumbling. (1 John 2:9-10)

The great theologian Tina Turner once famously sang, "What's love got to do with it?"

I'm pretty sure she didn't ask the question in quite the same context as John's words in chapter 2, but it's a valid question, even when you're not wearing a sparkly dress.

Apparently, love has everything to do with being a believer—it's one of the signs of assurance for the Christian.

I've heard pastors jokingly say, "I love ministry; I just don't love the people." I knew a guy who would lament his inability to experience significant community in the church while simultaneously quipping, "James, I just don't like people."

That's not funny. That's a problem.

Whoever says he is in the light and hates his brother is still in darkness.

Our love for one another is a sign we belong to God. Let me be clear. Our love for people doesn't earn love from God. God loves us. We love others. The order is important.

But one of the signs we are God's people is when we love people. God says it's pretty hard to praise him with our lips and then snub people made in his image (James 3:9-11). Maybe it's like someone saying they like me but can't stand my kids or my wife. Them's fightin' words.

Do you love people? Do you see people as God's finest creation? Do you want what is best for others? Do you care about the souls of the people you rub shoulders with on a daily basis? If the answer to any of these is "nope" --it's at least worth a conversation with their Maker.

Love is more than a catchy song lyric, a second-hand emotion, manufactured by sentimentality. It is a posture of the heart, an overflow of the love God showers on us. It is an intentional choice we make, not because we are forced to love, but because we love God.

Loving others is a sign you belong to God.

> Reflect:
>
> Do you love the people around you?
> How do you demonstrate your love for them?

Day 10

Forgiven

I am writing to you, little children, because your sins are forgiven for his name's sake. (1 John 2:12)

You are forgiven. Write that down. Circle it. Put a star next to it. Those are beautiful, life-giving words that we all need to hear.

Our sin is always a bigger deal than we think it is. Our little lies. Our grumbling hearts. Our selfish desires. Our envious attitudes. Our hurtful words. Our persistent pride. Our lustful desires. We all face sin sickness, and it's worse than we could ever imagine.

We often experience the horizontal consequences of sin: broken relationships, tarnished reputations, and suffocating heartache. We've been caught and confronted. We've been found out and called out. We've felt the weight of our sin and the heaviness of despair. But sin doesn't only have horizontal consequences. It does more than make relationships difficult. Sin separates us from God and brings death. It's no wonder that we've all longed to hear the words, "You are forgiven." The good news for you and me is those words have been spoken to us.

You are forgiven. Forgiveness is releasing someone from a debt that they owe and could never payback. Through

Christ's sinless death, God has forgiven your debt. Colossians 2 assures us God cancelled the record of debt and its legal demands of death by nailing it to the cross. He paid it off. He picked up the tab. That doesn't mean sin won't confront us, but it does mean it won't condemn us.

When the enemy tries to remind you of all the horrible things you've said, done, or thought over the years, remember, you are forgiven.

> Reflect:

> Thank God for the forgiveness He has given to you.

Day 11

I Know Someone Famous

I am writing to you, fathers, because you know him who is from the beginning. (1 John 2:13)

Do you know anyone famous?

I've *met* a few famous people, but I don't *know* any famous people.

I always thought it would be cool to know someone famous. If I knew a famous singer, I could get backstage passes to their concert. If I knew a famous athlete, I could get front row seats to the game. If I knew a famous person, I could tell everyone I know that I know someone famous and then I would become quasi-famous through association. I'd be famous once removed.

Just for fun, think of someone famous. Do you have a person in mind? Think about the benefits you might experience by being their friend. It would be cool, wouldn't it?

I have good news for you. You know someone famous. You know God. Better yet, God knows you. And because you know God, you have access to him. God is always accessible. Apparently, the fact that he rules and runs the world doesn't prevent a meeting at the drop of a hat.

Because of Christ, you have the sure promises of God. I've broken a promise before. I've told my kids we'd go somewhere or do something, and I've disappointed them. I've dropped the ball. It's not always intentional. Sometimes I just forget or sometimes, due to unforeseen, uncontrollable, unwelcome circumstances, I just can't do what I promised I would do. This never happens when God makes a promise. In fact, Paul says, "For all the promises of God find their Yes in [Christ Jesus]. (1 Corinthians 1:20)

You have the right to be called a child of God. You are God's kid, and God is pretty fond of his kids. He loves his sons and daughters. He loves you.

I am writing to you…because you know him who is from the beginning.

You know the Famous One.

Reflect:

What are some of the benefits of knowing God?

Day 12

We Won!

I am writing to you, young men, because you *have overcome the evil one. (1 John 2:13)*

We won! That's right, "We." I didn't play in the game. Technically (if you want to be technical), I wasn't on the team. But since my team won, *we* won.

The other year my favorite college team was in the NCAA tournament. They had a late game. Late for me is basically anything after 9 PM. Okay, 8.

I couldn't stay up, so I recorded the game. I woke up early on Sunday morning to watch the replay and found my oldest son watching downstairs, so I decided to join him.

As I watched the game unfold, it became obvious we were going to lose. I'll admit, I always feel this way unless it's mathematically impossible for the opposing team to win. But in this case, they really were going to lose

As precious seconds ticked away, my frustration and disappointment grew. With seconds left on the clock and the opposing team shooting free throws to ice the game, I stalked out of the room My team was going to lose. I was kicking myself for watching the game before I had to preach. Nobody likes an angry preacher!

As I walked out the door, my son said, "Dad, you might want to watch the end." It took all of .03 seconds for me to pivot and walk back in the room.

My son had already seen the score. He knew something that I didn't.

I can't tell you how quickly my mood changed when I saw the final score My team had won. We were victorious—and it changed everything.

If you're thinking about turning the channel on life, leaving the room, or grumbling in defeat-- you might want to watch to the end. We win.

I am writing to you . . . because you have overcome the evil one.

Reflect:

What does it mean to be victorious?
How does it change the way you live your life?

Day 13

Cotton Candy

Do not love the world or the things in the world....And the world is passing away along with its desires, but whoever does the will of God abides forever. (1 John 2:15)

Cotton candy is fun. It's even fun to say. Go ahead. Say it out loud. *Cotton candy.*

Admit it. You smiled just a little.

Cotton candy is fun to look at. It's fluffy like a colorful cloud you carry around on a stick. Who hasn't looked up to the sky and thought, "It sure would be nice if I could dye that cloud blue or pink, dip it in some sugar, wrap it around a stick, and eat it."

Sure, it gets a little sticky to the touch, but no one ever said, "Man, wish I didn't have to lick all this sugar off my face."

Despite its allure, cotton candy is arguably the most disappointing theme park food ever invented.

Cotton candy overpromises and underdelivers. Who has ever had cotton candy and immediately thought, "Boy, am I stuffed. I couldn't eat another bite. I'm going to put on my sweatpants." No one in the history of humankind has ever finished their miniature happy cloud on a stick and said out loud, "That really hit the spot."

The world is a lot like cotton candy. It's filled with eye candy-things that look fun and appealing that, once consumed, leave you longing for more. They are simply empty calories.

John warns us against the things of the world—the desires of the flesh, desires of the eyes, and the pride of possessions. In other words, our appetites, our affections, and our stuff. Pride, power, possessions, prestige, position… They promise to fill you with happiness and satisfaction, but they underdeliver. God promises they will pass away… kind of like cotton candy melting when it meets your tongue.

It's sobering for me.

John isn't suggesting that we shouldn't have desires, longings, or affections, but he is suggesting that those things shouldn't run contrary to Christ's desires and longings for us. They shouldn't fall in line with the world's system that defines success in life as upward mobility, cozy affluence, outward beauty, and temporary joy.

These are not from God, but the world.

So do not love the world or things of the world. Instead, consider a more satisfying alternative.

Reflect:

What are the pursuits in life that promise to satisfy?
How have you pursued them?
What have been the results?

Day 14

A Good Reminder

I write to you, not because you do not know the truth, but because you know it…(1 John 2:21)

Now that I'm over 40, I find myself forgetting things. I've caught myself a couple of times walking into a room and then forgetting why it was necessary to take the trip. Occasionally, I'll go to the grocery store with a mental list of three things to pick up. I'll come home with four items, and two of them weren't even on my list! Notes on my phone aren't just a helpful organizational tool, but a necessary aid in remembering what in the world I'm supposed to be doing. I even have found myself taking pictures of where I park in the airport parking garage so I don't spend the night aimlessly looking for my vehicle.

We all forget things. Sometimes, we forget important things. I've wondered to myself if that's one of the reasons Scripture so frequently reminds us of what we already know.

Sometimes I need to be reminded of what is true. I need to be told of wisdom I've already been taught. There are truths that Scripture declares that I've already heard, but I need to hear again. And again. And again. I think it's easy to read the whole of 1 John and come away thinking, "How many different ways can he think of to say the same thing over and over?" He seemed to understand our tendency to forget, and he wanted the truth to sink in deep.

Life with God isn't always about discovering a new truth, but remembering what we already know. John even says in chapter 2 verse 1: "Beloved, I am writing you no new commandment, but an old commandment that you had from the beginning." Some may see that as antiquated, old, or boring. I find it reassuring. Today, be reminded of what you already know. Search the Bible for age-old truth, and, if you need extra help remembering it, that's ok. Write it down or take a picture.

I write to you, not because you do not know the truth, but because you know it...

Reflect:

Is there an old truth that I need to be reminded of today?

Day 15

Gullible

I write these things to you about those who are trying to deceive you (1 John 2:26)

I once bought a stereo system out of the backseat of some guy's car. I know. Don't say it. It wasn't one of my finer moments. I was young(er), but old enough to vote, get married, and claim a child or two on my taxes.

I'm ashamed to tell the story, but it's important you remember, in my defense, the guy had a brochure and was a very good salesman.

He received a shipment of equipment for a customer (lie!) who no longer needed it (lie!) and unfortunately, he couldn't send it back (all lies!). For a couple hundred dollars I could have the whole surround sound system. The speakers. The sound bar. The projector. All mine. Wow! What a deal!

The guy had everything you need to run a good ~~business~~ scam. He had a slick website. He had a glossy business card. And, most importantly, he had a starry-eyed sucker (that was me).

I didn't have cash on me, so I told him I needed to drive to the bank to get money. (Trust me, I know this makes it worse). As I drove to the bank to withdraw my dignity from the ATM, all sorts of sirens sounded off in my still-underdeveloped brain. Did I mention he had a brochure? I mean, the guy didn't open his trench coat to show me watches hanging in rows. He had a business card and a fancy website. What could possibly go wrong?

In my defense (of which I have none), during that drive, I had serious doubts about our original agreement. But I still didn't have the wisdom to completely walk away. He left with my hard-earned $200, and I left with a valuable lesson: Don't believe everything you hear, read, or even see.

John puts it this way:

I write these things to you about those who are trying to deceive you…

It should come as no surprise that people have been teaching things about Jesus for some time that just aren't true. They may even have a brochure, a slick website, and a podcast. They unquestionably believe in their product, and lack no sincerity.

Be careful. Slick communication does not a solid doctrine (or reliable stereo system) make.

Do you want to know if someone is selling you a spiritual lie? Look at what they teach about Jesus. Start there. Stay there awhile, and examine it deeply against Scripture. It's wise to have a healthy dose of skepticism when it comes to biblical teaching. (Not cynicism; that would be sinful.) In Acts 17:11, Paul describes the Bereans as having "noble character." Why was that? He was impressed because they were "examining the Scriptures daily to see if these things were so." They didn't rely on Paul's credentials or reputation alone but compared his preaching with what they themselves found in Scriptures. Far from being offended that they doubted him, Paul praised them for their diligence.

Search the Word to see whether one's teaching about the Word is actually taught in the Word. I don't say this to frighten you, but to prepare you.

Mark the words of the once-suckered: There will be those who try to sell you something costly that has no value.

Reflect:

Have you ever been fooled?
How did you feel knowing you fell for something so foolish?
How can you prepare to identify false teaching?

Day 16

Abide

And now, little children, abide in him… (1 John 2:28)

Abide in Christ. Abiding is one of those spiritual ideas that we talk about in church, but we don't always know what it means practically. What does it mean to abide in Christ?

This isn't the first time John writes about this idea. In the Gospel of John, Jesus said:

"Abide in me, and I in you. As the branch cannot bear fruit by itself, unless it abides in the vine, neither can you, unless you abide in me. I am the vine; you are the branches. Whoever abides in me and I in him, he it is that bears much fruit, for apart from me you can do nothing. . .As the Father has loved me, so have I loved you. Abide in my love. If you keep my commandments, you will abide in my love, just as I have kept my Father's commandments and abide in his love. These things I have spoken to you, that my joy may be in you, and that your joy may be full. (John 15:4-5, 9-11)

John uses a metaphor of a vine and branches. Abiding in Christ is staying connected to the life-giving vine—Jesus.

What does that mean? Think of it this way: In the Christian life we experience *union* with Christ and *communion* with

Christ. They are not the same thing. One flows out of the other. In faith, we are united with Christ much like a husband and wife are united in marriage. But union doesn't always guarantee connection. If someone asked you, "How is your marriage?" you wouldn't respond, "We're legally married." If someone asked you, "How's your relationship with your husband?" you wouldn't say, "He claimed me on his taxes last year." Ideally, you want union and communion working in harmony.

In the same way, we can be united to Christ, but not experience communion with Christ. Abiding is a relationship word meaning to dwell, or stay, or remain in the same place. We are to remain in relationship with Christ. It is going to Christ to receive what He continually gives. Abiding in Christ isn't about changing your status with Christ but living in communion with Christ. Abiding isn't producing something you don't have as much as it is enjoying someone you do have. Abiding is the act of receiving all that God is for us in Christ. It is believing and trusting in Christ.

Reflect?

What would it look like for you to abide in Christ today?

Day 17

Confidence at His Coming

And now, little children, abide in him, so that when he appears we may have confidence and not shrink from him in shame at his coming. (1 John 2:28)

When it came to my mess-ups as a kid, there were what I'd call misdemeanors and felonies.

Misdemeanors were handled by mom. This was when I had to go to my room to "think about what I had done." As far as punishments go, this wasn't so bad. For the most part, thinking didn't hurt.

Then there were the behavioral felonies—acts so egregious that mom would have to involve dad. I never liked hearing those dreaded words: "You wait until your father gets home!" This meant that I had made my mother so mad, I deserved something worse than "thinking."

When I heard those words, I usually felt (in this order) fear and guilt. Full disclosure, guilt was late to the party. I was afraid because I knew my dad would discipline me, and it would likely sting. To a lesser degree, I also experienced guilt, knowing I'd done wrong.

When we're connected to Christ, John reassures believers that we need not feel shame or shrink back at the thought of him coming home. He's not coming back to punish us.

How is that even possible? It's certainly not because of our stellar record. No matter who we are, compared to a holy God, our resume of righteousness is far from impressive.

Our confidence stands because Christ is our righteous one. As the author of Hebrews writes, *"...so Christ, having been offered once to bear the sins of many, will appear a second time, not to deal with sin but to save those who are eagerly waiting for him."* His constant intercession on our behalf guarantees that God doesn't turn away from us. In Christ, He has moved toward us. This is good news.

When he appears we may have confidence and not shrink from him in shame at his coming.

So, rest assured. Be confident. Experience his peace. Wait until your Father gets home—but not so he can dole out the penalties for your felonies (or misdemeanors). Those have already been paid for by Christ.

Reflect:

Do you have confidence when you think about seeing Jesus? Why or why not?

Day 18

lavish: to expend or bestow profusely

See what great love the Father has lavished on us (1 John 3:1)

Several years ago, I met a man who changed my life. The first time I sat down with him for breakfast, he offered to send me to Israel. I didn't know him. He didn't know me. For some strange reason that I still don't fully understand, he saw fit to give me a gift I had not earned nor deserved.

Sometime later, when he heard that an unexpected heart procedure and unplanned home repairs crippled our family with debt, he paid it off. I still remember walking to the mailbox, pulling out the unfamiliar envelope, and opening it up to find a check that took my breath away. I sat on the porch holding the check while weeping. My wife, Melissa, finally came outside only to find me undone.

When I called him, I said through tears, "You don't even know me." He said, "I don't have to know you. I love you." You can't see me now, but even as I write this, my eyes well up with tears.

It didn't stop there. His generosity has continued. Each year he has sent my wife and I away on vacation, just the two of us. It's been life giving for us as a couple. When we return from a trip he asks, "Where to next?" All of this is completely undeserved. A man who didn't know me from Adam has treated me like a favored son.

What is truly beautiful about this story is that one man's lavish generosity has reminded me of God's lavish grace. You may read this and think to yourself, "I wish that were me!" I have good news for you. It is you. God lavishly pours out this kind of love every day. He's doing it right now. We only need to see it.

See what great love the Father has lavished on us...

Reflect

In what ways has God lavished his love upon you?

Day 19

Name Calling

See the great love the Father has lavished on us, that we should be called children of God; and so we are. (1 John 3:1)

When I was a kid, I was called names. I was an easy target. For starters, I wore goofy glasses. I heard "Four eyes!" a time or two. In elementary school, I was referred to as "husky." At least that's what my jeans called me, but I knew what that meant. Some of the names were more hurtful than others. I suspect I'm not the only one to be on the receiving end of a harmful name. We've all been called names. Even God has given you a name. He calls you his child.

You're God's kid, and He's crazy about you. As His son or daughter, you experience the unique privileges of being a child of God. As God's children, you experience:

Security. When I was a kid, my dad said, "It's going to be ok." I believed him. I know now this was a parenting trick to sooth my uncertainty, but with God, it's 100% true. As a child of God, you are secure. Even in the midst of very real problems, your future hope is secure.

Intimacy. A child's relationship with his or her parent is different than any other relationship. I've met a lot of cool kids. I've enjoyed my fair share of conversations with kids, and I've left many conversations thinking, "That's a cool kid!" But there are only three kids I leave a conversation with and say, "That's *my* kid." As a child of God, you have intimacy with your Father.

Inheritance. Someday, my children are going to inherit my massive fortune (I don't have a massive fortune. Truthfully, I don't even have a fortune). Regardless, what I have now will be theirs. What God has is yours. Think about that for a minute! As a child of God, you receive the riches of Christ Jesus.

God is calling you, but He's not calling you names. He calls you his own.

Reflect:

What are the benefits of being a child of God?

Day 20

The Best is Yet to Come

Beloved, we are God's children now, and what we will be has not yet appeared; but we know that when he appears we shall be like him, because we shall see him as he is." (1 John 3:2)

On a hot summer day in July I was walking my then 88-year-old grandma out to her car. As we approached her vehicle, I turned to her and asked, "Grandma, how are you feeling?" She stopped walking, looked me in the eye, and said, "James, I'm not what I once was." She paused, smiled, and continued, "But I'm not yet what I will be." Who says that?! I'd like to think it was original to my grandma, but it wasn't.

Beloved, we are God's children now, and what we will be has not yet appeared; but we know that when he appears we shall be like him, because we shall see him as he is.

The best is yet to come. That's good news when you're growing old and feeling weary. It's good news when you fight sickness or are dealt a debilitating disease. It's good news when relationships come crashing down and hardship comes crashing in. It's even good news when life brings joy. This life isn't as good as it gets. At its very best, this world is only an appetizer to the main course. And when life's circumstances are at their worst, remember, the world will not have the final say.

We may not be what we were, but we're not yet what we will be. The best is yet to come.

Reflect:

What will it be like to "be like Him"?

Day 21

Who Does He *Act* Like?

But we know that when he appears we shall be like him, because we shall see him as he is." (1 John 3:2b)

The first question my mother asks when a child is born is, "Who does he look like?" This always confuses me. Babies have a unique look. They're squishy, cuddly and have a unique baby smell. It's hard to compare a baby with a guy in his 30s who trims his beard and smells like, well, not like a baby. As much as I hate to admit it, mom was on to something. Kids look like their parents. You may look like your mother or father, but one day you'll perfectly reflect the Son.

We know from 1 John 3:1 that when Jesus appears, we will be like him. Sometimes we confuse being like Jesus with *being* Jesus. We're not Jesus. He's one of a kind. It never ends well when we play a role that's already cast. He doesn't need us to sit in his seat or hold his place in the front of the line. Even though we're not called to be Jesus, we are called to be *like* Jesus. We should reflect Jesus in how we think and act.

Thinking and acting like Jesus can be overwhelming. If we're honest, we must admit we fall woefully short. The whole sinless bit is a hard act to follow. But as we imperfectly pursue the Perfect One, we can make another mistake, too. We can assume the presence of sin in our lives means we have no power over sin. We believe that we are who we are. We take it at face value that we're never going to change. That's not just unfortunate, but unbiblical. God is changing us. *"And we all, with unveiled face, beholding the glory of the Lord, are being transformed into the same image from one degree of glory to another." (2 Corinthians 3:18)*

God is in the business of changing people. He does it all the time. He turns persecutors into preachers, scared fishermen into bold disciples, and crooks into Christ-followers. God has done this throughout time, and he's doing it right now in you. So, go ahead, reflect your Father.

Reflect:

How is God changing the way you reflect Jesus?

Day 22

Practice Makes…

Everyone who makes a practice of sinning also practices lawlessness…Whoever practices righteousness is righteous, as He is righteous (1 John 3:4; 7)

Practice makes perfect. That's a lie. Nothing could be further from the truth. Have you seen me swing a golf club? My friend tells me I golf like an 80-year-old man. When I hear him say that, I think, "That old guy must be a pretty good golfer." A few years ago, when I was golfing with my friend, we approached a 180-yard par 3. I looked at my bag, pulled out my driver, and teed it up. I left it short. I've been practicing my golf swing for 25 years and even still, it's far from perfect.

While practice doesn't make you perfect, what you practice reveals something about the person you're becoming. Practice sin and you will produce lawlessness. Cut corners, cover-up, and conceal, and your character will be revealed. It won't be pretty.

But there's good news.

Whoever practices righteousness is righteous.

Notice that John doesn't say, "Whoever practices righteousness will become righteous." This is important.

The Christian life isn't about becoming something you're not as much as it is living out something that you are. If you're a child of God, the righteousness of Christ is yours. That doesn't mean we don't desire to grow in Christlikeness. It doesn't mean that we won't pursue holiness. We certainly do! Practicing righteousness reveals our standing before God, but it doesn't earn our standing before God. Practice doesn't produce perfection. Practice reveals character.

Reflect:

In your life with God, what are you practicing? What does this communicate about what you value?

Day 23

Costly Love

By this we know love, that he laid down his life for us, and we ought to lay down our lives for the brothers. (1 John 3:16)

Have you ever been loved? Has some knight in shining armor showed up at your doorstep on his trusty steed (or Honda Civic) bearing gifts? Did he woo you until he won you? Did some young lady catch your eye at freshman orientation? Did she write sweet notes and dot her i's with little hearts? Did she hold your hand until you finally fell for her?

I don't know how it happened for you, but if it has happened, then you have experienced love. Something tells me thinking about it brings a smile to your face. I also think if I asked you to explain love to my seven-year-old, you'd wrestle with finding the right words. How do you know love? According to John, you know love because Jesus demonstrated love.

By this we know love, that he laid down his life for us…

This isn't "butterflies in the stomach" love. This love isn't "lost in the clouds" love or "I just think he's so cute" love. This is sacrificial love. It is extravagant love. God's love for us is logic defying love. How do we know love? Look to Jesus. His love was on full display on a criminal's cross. He held nothing back. He spared no expense. He laid down his life to redeem his brothers and sisters. This is God's costly love.

This radical, self-giving love is what we are called to give to others. "And we ought to lay down our lives for the brothers." That's a high bar. I'm not a fan of sharing my last piece of pie let alone my life. Yet, this is the love we have come to know. And because we have experienced this love in Christ, we are now called to extend it to our brothers and sisters. You've been loved. Now love one another.

Reflect:

How do you love your brothers and sisters?
How is it similar or dissimilar to the love of Christ?

Day 24

Love Has Legs

But if anyone has the world's goods and sees his brother in need, yet closes his heart against him, how does God's love abide in Him? Little children, let us not love in word or talk but in deed…(1 John 3:17-18)

Talk is cheap, but love is costly because love does. If love doesn't do anything, if it's good intentions and no follow through, all talk and no walk, then it's not love. It may be an idea. It may even be a good idea, but if it doesn't have legs, it's not love. Love has some Missouri in it. Missouri is the "show me" state. Saying "I love you" without showing "I love you" is empty. You may wax eloquently about love, but if you don't show love, your words will melt away like Olaf in the heat of summer.

How do we love? John tell us one practical way is by helping those in need.

But if anyone has the world's goods and sees his brother in need, yet closes his heart against him, how does God's love abide in Him?

Do you hear the seriousness of that? John says if you have the means to help someone in need and choose to ignore them anyway, how can God's love abide in you? Does this mean we have to help everyone? By no means! While you will not be able to help everyone, you can help someone. Love the person in front of you. Don't run your mouth about loving. Run over and help a brother out. Words and talk are just that. Love has legs.

Reflect:

Look around. Do you see someone in need? What are you waiting for?

Day 25

Speaking the Truth in Love

Little children, let us not love in word or talk but in deed and in truth (1 John 3:18)

My kid was chasing a ball into a busy intersection the other day, cars speeding everywhere. I didn't say anything. He had a smile on his face and seemed like he was having so much fun!

That didn't happen. But if it did, you would question whether I should be allowed to have children in my care.

That's not love. Allowing a child to engage in risky behavior simply because he enjoys it is not loving. In the same way, sometimes love is speaking up even if our words won't be well received in the moment. My friend Billy once told me, "If I ever find out that you know something about me that I need to hear, and you don't tell me, I'd be crushed." In other words, sometimes the most loving thing we can do is to speak the truth…in love (see Ephesians 4:15).

Admittedly, it doesn't always feel loving to tell the truth because sometimes it's not. When it lacks the indispensable *love* element, truth-telling becomes vindictive and cruel.

Like hydrogen peroxide on an open wound, even truth shared in love can sting. That's why when I'm on the receiving end of words that make me wince, I assume there is at least some truth in what is being said. I may not agree with everything. I may not *like* everything. But I know a) I have blind spots and b) I've asked God to help me see them, even if it means a blow to my ego.

Maturity in Christ involves the humility to receive truth spoken in love and the courage to deliver it compassionately.

Like letting our kids traipse in the path of a Mack truck, it's not loving to passively keep our mouths shut when we should open them. Our goal isn't to be harmful, but to be helpful with our words: "Let no corrupting talk come out of your mouths, but only such as is good for building up, as fits the occasion, that it may give grace to those who hear" (Ephesians 4:29).

Sadly, love is often defined as acceptance at all costs, but sometimes, if we truly love, we need to be truthful at all costs

Reflect:

Do you need to have a truthful conversation with someone you love? When will you?

Day 26

We Good, God?

By this we shall know that we are of the truth and reassure our hearts before him; for whenever our heart condemns us, God is greater than our heart, and he knows everything. (1 John 3:19)

Sometimes I'll think something is wrong in my marriage when nothing is wrong. It's my own insecurity. Or maybe I simply miss the signals. Sometimes I'll ask my sweet Melissa, "Are we good?"

She'll smile and respond, "Yep."

But I'll still wonder so I'll follow up my question with another, totally different question. "So, we're good?"

She'll smile and say, "Yes, James, we're good."

Still not fully convinced, I'll ask one more time, "You're sure we're good?"

She'll smile. "James, we're good, but if you ask me one more time if we're good we're not going to be good." We'll laugh.

I'm slow and sometimes need to be reassured. Maybe you're like me. Have you wondered if you're good with God? Maybe you've wondered if he's mad at you or ready to drop the hammer on you. Or maybe you doubt his love or his presence.

Do you know how you can know if you're good with God?

Listen to the Word and don't let your emotions run the show. Just like my instincts can run amuck in the what ifs, my heart can mislead me. It can't always be trusted. There's something more trustworthy than my fickle feelings—God's spoken word.

Instead of following your heart, remember that what God says is always true above what you feel.

Reflect:

How do you respond to fickle feelings in faith?

Day 27

The Love of God Goes Public

In this the love of God was made manifest among us, that God sent his only Son into the world. (1 John 4:9)

When I was in high school, public displays of affection were frowned upon. Warnings against PDA were written in the school handbook that nobody read. You were there to learn, not fall in love. Students with raging hormones were discouraged from playing kissy-face in the halls. Students were highly encouraged to keep their feelings (and hands) to themselves. God does not share the same desire to avoid public displays of affection.

. . . the love of God was made manifest among us, that God sent his only Son into the world.

God's love was made visible. It was not hidden. *Manifest* means to put on display or to make visible. Think Clark Griswold's Christmas lights flooding the dark December night sky.

God's love for you was displayed for the world to see in the humble form of Jesus. His Son was the ultimate public display of affection.

Reflect:

List a few ways you've seen God's love demonstrated in your life.

Day 28

Consider the Source

In this is love, not that we have loved God but that he loved us and sent his Son to be the propitiation for our sins. (1 John 4:10)

I pursued my wife. I think I chased her until she simply surrendered in exhaustion. I was like a cheetah chasing after a gazelle. In my mind, she was playing hard to get. You know, making me work a bit. What she really wanted was for me to initiate. She still does.

Sometimes we forget that God loved us first. He initiated. Our relationship with God started because of God. We didn't wise up after carefully weighing the pros and cons of following Christ. We didn't chase after God like I chased after Melissa. We didn't sprint our way to the Spirit. God loved us first.

God didn't love us because we were incredibly lovable. We didn't win him over with our smile or sense of humor. We weren't really all that attractive. As a matter of fact, we didn't love God at all. Let that sink in for a second. We didn't love God.

Scripture teaches that our sin separates us from God. It therefore seems logical that if reconciliation between God and man is going to happen, it should start with the offending party. That's you and me. After all, we are the ones who caused the problem in the first place. This is how it works in the world. You offend me, hurt me, disappoint me, or sin against me and I'll pull back and wait for an apology. But God knew if reconciliation was going to happen, it would have to start with him. And so, he initiated. While we were still separated, still lost in sin, he sent his Son—the perfect man—the only one whose death could satisfy our debt to sin and bring us to God.

In this is love, not that we have loved God but that he loved us and sent his Son to be the propitiation for our sins.

When our kids disobey, we may be tempted to say, "You go to your room and think about what you've done. When you're ready to apologize you know where to find me. I'll wait." But God did not stand a distance and say, "I'll wait." God sent. God sent Jesus. God sent love.

Reflect:

How does it feel to be pursued by a perfect and loving Father?

Day 29

Obedience Isn't a Burden

For this is the love of God, that we keep his commandments. And his commandments are not burdensome. (1 John 5:3)

Do you remember the first time as a kid you decided you were not a big fan of the rules? You were told to clean your room, but you didn't like cleaning your room. You knew you were supposed to put your dirty laundry in the basket, but you weren't a fan of laundry. You knew that your job was to empty the dishwasher, but it seemed excessive and unkind to ask a kid to do such hard labor. And why should you have to mow the lawn when you weren't the one who sent the rain and made it grow!?

All of those rules seemed like unnecessary weights placed unfairly upon your shoulders. In fact, following all those rules was suffocating to your own personal freedom. They were hindrances to the life of joy that you longed to experience.

To those who are hesitant to cooperate (that's all of us), John writes these convicting words:

For this is the love of God, that we keep his commandments. And his commandments are not burdensome.

Loving God is connected to obeying God. We love God and obey his commands. Loving God doesn't mean thoughtfully considering and contemplating the commands of God, but actually doing what he says. Obedience is the appropriate response to the love God has lavished on us and a result of a deepening love we have for him. The more you know God and love him, the more you will love his commands and desire to obey them.

Almost every day I ask my daughter to snuggle. What dad doesn't want to snuggle with his daughter? Recently, she has decided it's funny when I ask her if she wants to snuggle. She will politely reply, "No, thank you" and walk away. Can you imagine if we did this whenever someone we love asked us to lend a hand?

Sweetie, can you empty the dishwasher? "No."
Love, can you grab my phone when you're downstairs? "Nope."
Honey, can pick me up a gallon of milk while you're at the store? "I don't think so."

That doesn't sound very loving, does it? It doesn't sound loving because it's not loving.

Because we love God and have been empowered by the Spirit of God, we delight in keeping the commands of God. And his commands are not burdensome. They are not unnecessary weights placed upon our shoulders meant to steal our joy. God's commands are not meant to be a beat down, but a delight. They do not hinder our joy but protect us from evil. "Therefore I love your commandments above gold, above fine gold." (Psalm 119:27)

For this is the love of God, that we keep his commandments. And his commandments are not burdensome.

Reflect?

Is there a particular command God is calling you to obey today?

Day 30

Ask Anything

And this is the confidence that we have toward him, that if we ask anything according to his will he hears us. And if we know that he hears us in whatever we ask, we know that we have the requests that we have asked of him. (1 John 5:14-15)

"If God were to answer all your prayers, would you even know it?" When my friend Cliff asked a room full of church goers that question, I felt conviction. I tend to pray safe prayers or broad prayers. "Bless this or that" or "Watch over him or her." My prayer life can be so clouded with generalities that I'm not always sure when, or if, God specifically answers. Or, worse, sometimes I'm just not sure what to ask for, so I don't ask for anything.

Think about what John is saying in these verses. If we ask anything according to God's will, he hears us. Sometimes using the phrase "according to His will" gets a bad rap. Some people think we're giving God an out. We know what we really want, but we're afraid God will say "No" and we don't want to explain to our friends why God didn't answer in the affirmative. So, just to be safe, we tag "if it's your will" to the beginning or end of our prayer so God doesn't feel any unnecessary pressure.

God doesn't need us to cover for him. He can handle it. Praying according to the will of God isn't showing a lack of faith. It's showing that God is sovereign and we're not. It's believing God knows what's best and will do what's best. We humbly admit our proper place as the created and not the Creator. Jesus himself prayed this way in the Garden: "Father, if you are willing, remove this cup from me. Nevertheless, not my will, but yours, be done." (Luke 22:42-43)

What is beautiful about humbly asking God to work according to His will is that He will actually do it. God answered Jesus' garden request, "My Son, you will need to drink from this cup. It is my will that you taste death." And so he did.

And if we know that he hears us in whatever we ask, we know that we have the requests that we have asked of him.

So, go ahead, pray big, audacious prayers. Ask God for what's on your heart. Ask God for his will to be done. And ask God for the desire to see his will done, no matter the answer. Then watch him do it.

Reflect:

What are you praying about right now?

Day 31

American Idol

Little children, keep yourselves from idols. (1 John 5:21)

I'm trying to remember my parents' last words as I went off to college.

I'm not positive, but they were probably along the lines of "I love you" or "I'm proud of you" or "Work hard" or "Remember, you don't have a job or money so spend accordingly." Either way, their last words were encouraging, uplifting, and wise.

Do you know what my parents didn't say as I backed out of my driveway? They didn't say, "Keep yourself from idols!"

But these were John's last words.

When I think of idols, I think of some cool stone cat sitting crisscross-applesauce with an extra eye on his forehead. But I'm not sure that's what John had in mind. An idol doesn't have to sit in a prominent position on your fireplace. It just needs a place in your heart.

An idol is anything that takes God's seat in our hearts and minds.

Want to identify your idols? Try this: Take them away and see how you respond.

Does the thought of losing your title at work crush you? Do you suffer sleepless nights when your stocks go down a few percentage points? How do you feel when your kids don't make the honor roll, let in the game winning goal, or are overlooked at the end of year banquet? I can make an idol of my reputation, my accomplishments, my income, my possessions, my retirement account, my spouse, my kids. Honestly, that's just scratching the idol surface.

The thing about idols is they never satisfy our restless hearts. The public praise we long for lifts our soul for a second before we're looking for the next fix. The new trinket that tickles our fancy when it arrives at our doorstep quickly seems "less than" when the new version of the same trinket is released. The grass at the new house still needs to be mowed; the new car still needs new brakes; the dream job still calls for work to be done.

Idols never fully satisfy our souls, but that's not the biggest issue. If it was, we'd just live life like Goldilocks. We'd move from one experience to the next, thinking there's something better to be discovered--a more filling food or more pleasurable place. No, idolatry isn't only a satisfaction problem, it's a savior problem. It's when we look to something or someone other than Jesus to save us. It's trusting, following or exalting anyone or anything above Jesus. He said, "I am the bread of life; whoever comes to me shall not hunger, and whoever believes in me shall never thirst." (John 6:35)

It's no wonder John's last words are a command. *Keep yourself from idols.*

Reflect:

What captivates my heart so much that if I lost it, I would be devastated?

Made in the USA
Middletown, DE
09 May 2022